THE TALKING DRUM

POEMS BY KEITH FLYNN

© 1991, 1996 by Keith Flynn.
All rights reserved.
Printed in the United States of America.
Second edition.

Manufactured by Professional Press,
Jerry Cooper, PO Box 4371, Chapel Hill, NC.

Published by Animal Sounds,
PO Box 7086, Asheville, NC 28802.

ISBN 1-889276-00-6

Book design and typography by Lowell Allen,
62½ N. Lexington Avenue, Asheville, NC 28801.

Front cover illustration:
"Jamba"
by Townie New.

Back cover photo taken by W. Erik McDaniel,
New York City, 1995.

Grateful acknowledgement is made to the following publications
where many of these poems have previously appeared:
*Ark River Retrospectives, The Arts Journal, The Fury, New Arts
Review, The New Press, Now and Then, Passages Northwest.*

The Talking Drum was originally published in 1991
by Metropolis Communications, Nashville, TN.

For Bill,

ANIMAL
SOUNDS

All Best
in the New
World Order,

— Keith Flynn

▲▲▲
THE LIE
▼▼▼

Planting 8
Walkabout 9
The Great Book 10
The Island Of The Body 11
Miracle Play 12
Chugach Conversion 13
The Anniversary Of The Fall 14
Genius Loci 15
The Lie 17
Pilgrim 20

▲▲▲
THE ZOO
▼▼▼

Koko 22
Year Of The Snake 24
Teenage Mutant Ninja Turtles 25
Noah 26
Elephant Graveyard 27
The Blue Hole 29
Eden Again 36
The Orchard and The Lash 37
The Horses 38
The Mind As Falcon 40

▲▲▲

THE ASTROLOGY OF LONGING

▼▼▼

The Door 42
Quickly Now The Crowd 43
Diorama 44
Adultery 45
With A Few Sticks 46
Midlothian 47
Echoes 48
Icons Between Classes 49
Irezumi 50
Vanilla 51

▲▲▲

WHERE THE WATER GOES

▼▼▼

Words For The Dying 56
Vertigo 57
The Girl Next Door All Grown Up . . . 59
To My Teacher At 50 61
Castro's Ghost 62
Dream Trail 64
Twilight In Brooklyn 65
Where The Water Goes 67

for my Mother

THE LIE

"The earth, for example, has often been a lie,

And the wind its rumor.

Together once, they drove all
The better people away."

"Oklahoma"
—*Larry Levis*

PLANTING

On the warmest part of my hair
a butterfly landed,
left blue on my cheek.
The dirt road facing the house
piles rocks in its middle
like a spine.

Once, with the dog days of August
breathing in their windows,
some boys fueled their father's truck
and roared, spewing rock
from shoulder to shoulder,
planting nothing.

But when they met asphalt,
the dog, sensing something
beyond spirals of heat
and crazed intervals of rain,
faced the swirling road,
like a movie reel run backward,
and leaped from the bouncing truck.

Blood and hair scattered like quilt
across double yellow line
by the mailbox of Old Man Reece.
Potatoes slept in their shells,
tucked in the soft dirt
behind the dam of rusted cars
directing the creek.

A '43 Ford with the windshield
still intact, reflected clouds
like cauliflower pushing west.
Their father said, clean the road
with shovels, and they scooped dog
into the water, again planting nothing.

An old dog anyway, they said,
minnows moving like pins
through his muddy eyes.
In the shadow of the black barn
that faced the creek, rage-red wasps
bored burrows into the wood.
Suicide bombers protecting a paper house.

West say the clouds west.

WALKABOUT

There is a story if you corner a scorpion,
that it will kill itself,
plant the poisonous tip
deep in its own back
before the tormentors may decide a fate.
But I have seen scorpions alive in a box.
Rage breeds many things.

The scorpion knows what it is.
Men in blue uniforms demanded my fingerprint,
staining my hands and shirt with ink.
In the bathroom,
I touched the mirror
where my face belonged.
I smudged a mustache on the reflection
that grew to darken the room.

On my thumb the lines whirl
in upon themselves down to a middle
and spreading are lost
to skin hair blood bone.
Buying cigarettes, I came up short,
dropping the faces of quarters
worn thin by thumbs, on the glass counter,
one at a time.

In the shower I watch my body change colors.
Chairs shrink as I approach.
Last night, I stumbled home,
thinking a naked black tree was God.
I imagined the roots sucking
for the shine of water
and I saw the silver glint
of lives slanting away.

A man and a woman were coiled in my bed.
Water splashed toward the sea
from my sink and the light
lunged at everything.
I was drunk and alone
and I stabbed at the lamp with a pencil
until the gray figures fascinated
shivered words. Move over.
Give me room. Relax.
As if there was more than one reason to love.

THE GREAT BOOK

They will say it took only seven days.
They will say that the sky broke open
and made a sailor of an old drunk
who spoke to animals
and won a rainbow lottery from God.
They will tell you of a reluctant prophet
swallowed by a giant fish,
who lounged in his lawn chair,
until tired of the cruise,
he was spit upon the beach.
They will talk about Jesus,
flying like a fat bee from the tomb,
showing off the scratches he got
from fucking around on somebody's turf.
O they will talk about murders & miracles.
They will show you heads on platters
and a busybody that turned into a salt statue.
But hey, that's cool,
there are other lights to be seen
as you swim slowly homeward
and you say,
I didn't choose this profession,
it chose me.
And there will be no Coney Island,
no government official to size you up,
no gross misconduct,
only one great book as big as a car,
with a shovel for a place marker.
Inside will be your name and a map,
and when you find the giant X
on the other side of the island,
you'll think THIS IS IT
and you'll dig...
and dig...
and dig...

The Island Of The Body

Stranded on the island of the body,
the spirit flies solo,
a medicine wheel launched into space,
one long improvisation
testing the stations of acceptance,
struggling to communicate,
in strangled phrases,
the praises of privileged light,
leaving a smoke stain
on the lantern of escape.

The years unsnarl themselves,
bad nerves, Benzedrine, nightmare analysis,
the spokes of memory knitted into strength.
The diary of a hollow horse is composed,
smiling like a sphinx.
Imaginary brides are stripped,
all limbs and lips open for suggestion,
roaming the landscape lost in thought,
like petals dropped behind in a pond.

With much grumbling, a grave is dug,
a house is made, miracles shoveled in a pile.
The family ghost settles in,
sick of bullets and bells, monkey gossip,
all this mosquito love.
Silence is purchased
with a housewife's critical eye
and nothing dies except rebellion.
The tide rolls up, the flowers forget their poetry.
Puritan sensibilities crouch naked in the trees.

MIRACLE PLAY

It might remain delicate
to the eye
if I cushion it right

and said of all the wrongs this
was nothing
major. No one had died

and besides I told
your brother
man the bag lady that

squatted on the corner smiling
dressed in green
disappeared today. I mean talking

to a friend from the flat
upstairs and
just vanished in front of him.

Two walking up a hill
and one stays
one becomes the sky.

How may anyone discern the way
the leaves breathe
in living light? I mean does

it matter that you bought a
shaved antler
and called it a genuine Iroquois

knife and then sneezed all
the coke off
your mirror? O there is music in

circumstance and dual flesh
clutters all
the pictures of eternity. How much

depends upon a disappearing bag lady?
Of all the
cries her was the least.

But she smelled fish frying
and knew the orchid
and wasn't made to die.

Chugach Conversion

His brother said God was east,
in Bristol,
in the soccer stadium shaking hands
and putting an end to mumbo jumbo.
Takeshi didn't believe him,
refused to believe him.

Look at the cedar, the hemlock greening.
The mink runs to our traps.
You will see.
You will.
God sits north in the great land.

They set off away from the inlet,
past an Aleut cursing on the cement,
handcuffed to a parking meter.
Halibut canneries watched them slog
into the Chugach range,
deceptively warm.

Takeshi seemed asleep when his brother
turned to the city running,
sure that Takeshi had seen God,
convinced he had seen Him.
His face covered the sky
and light leaked through His hair.

The AP wire was less spectacular.

Takeshi Nishimura of Kodiak
frozen under a birch in east Anchorage.

THE ANNIVERSARY OF THE FALL

The stunned populace grew hopeful.
The president's words were a soothing balm.
Everything is cool, he said, nothing to fear.
The Dow will calm itself in hours, silly thing.
Brokers tiptoed on their ledges,
pointing their toes into the carbon monoxide
morning & ticker tape curled from its metal tree
hissing, trust me, buy now, now is the time
for all good men to remember, remember.
One panic-stricken professor cawed,
million billion trillion zillion,
over & over, as he searched for the answer
to the Prime Number Theorem,
and the Jell-O dollar slipped like ice
into a sea of ink, Black was its color,
and Friday its proper name.
Stardust exponentials, paper before
and paper behind, one last heaping bowl
of soft peaches, couldn't hurt, they said,
couldn't hurt. Anyway, thank God for the FSLIC.
A man in Missouri shoots his wife & child
in the eye, turns the gun on himself,
murmuring Armageddon. So there.
You have my word on it.
I promise only to lie to you
when I have to.

Genius Loci

In the cove beyond the tunnel,
a secret place we needed, she said twenty,
and I nodded, thinking we were suddenly

very old or that the world was slowing.
I caressed the lamp of her belly
while Hendrix played on the tape deck,

crossing over to the other side.
Jimi was a voodoo child, she said,
saw through this red haze to the real.

I imagined him drowning as we washed
aimlessly through the car, offering sounds
that were ignored by the sky, with the stars

spinning & exploding. I heard Jimi strangling,
his fingers scratching at some piece of the air
to free him, something to hold in his hands

as firmly as a guitar. The creaking springs
of my seat were smothered in the enormous
rattle of planets changing their minds,

and the light between our thrusting bodies
and the moon became crowded with a grainy fog
and a waste. The fire we tried desperately

to make seemed to stray to the edges
and leave only a cinder, raw and cold
in the trees. In the end what we chose

was absence as we lay there naked
and a chill sliced between us, a greed
already eroding the other.

I thought of Hendrix drowned, of her drowned
in a thousand greasy hands, how our every act,
every song we conjured meant nothing,

had altered in no way the evening's scorched
replies. I drove from there with her,
drove all night as the heavens stormed & choked,

until I found her apartment and left
a pathetic kiss, while the clouds gathered
and gathered and nothing ever broke.

THE LIE

"Go soul, the body's guest,
Upon a thankless errand;
Fear not to touch the best;
The truth shall be thy warrant.
Go, since I must needs die,
And give the world the lie."

—Sir Walter Raleigh

So this is how the world looks
when a man subsides.
Sloshing brain-sick as a cantaloupe,
I sway in the pendulum of my chair,
chatting with my childhood friend,
for whose existence
I endured the mockery of my father.
I have lived my whole life
and I am still alive.
Stranger pastures like tents unfolding,
I have confused the tedious decisions.
I have embraced the sapphire's legacy
and been imprisoned by rooms
of perfumed satin.
I continued silent investigations.
From this I learned to worship
the shade beneath stones.

But now, when I sit, my chest sags
like the breasts of a woman.
I have turned inside out like a glove,
all the destitute regions of my body
surface, my falling hair,
my puckered corroding face.
Here and there light changes my posture.
Before I sleep, I shiver like meringue
and construct the museum of myself,
my teeth, my glasses, my cane,
on a night-stand by the bed.
Bruises appear mysteriously while I dream
and *I am still alive.*

◆

Seasoned in suspicion, I consider
Picasso's smooth blue woman
hanging on my wall,
crying in the creamy light of her room.
I imagine her watching a star,
thick as milk, fatten and fall from the sky,
splashing on a black Angus calf
being drug from the womb,
making a diamond between its eyes
as it hobbled clumsy through the barn
and raised its moon face to drink
in one tear from a hole in the darkness.

I imagine God, the Indian-giver,
giving back the Flood
and all the children outwitting Him,
learning to breathe underwater
as the moon splintered
and washed over them,
filling their lungs and eyes
with quills of light,
their every movement a rebellion
against the lie.

◆

From my closet, an empty coat calls my name.
I drink the sound of death down
like a flame and I am still alive.
I hear him everywhere.
I am accustomed to finding him
in the middle of the highway,
acting nonchalant, his thumb out,
no bags at his feet.

When the magazine vendor thrusts the paper
in my face, I see death dressed as a president,
as a farm hand, in picture after picture,
a pig-tailed girl on her bike sells doughnuts
for a beautification drive and yet,
her freckled face is spotted
with the residue of death.

There is no solace in the neighbor's son
as he plays tag with his dog,
tossing a green frisbee and giggling.
It seems such isolated joy
until I stagger inside for a beer
and return to find the boy
poking his puppy in the eye with a straw.

◆

On Friday I lunch with the resilient undergrad
who quotes Donne, and shows me the earrings
she has stolen from Bon Marche.
We order grilled cheese at the diner
and she becomes a flat-chested waitress
staggering under seven plates
on a five-plate tray.
She feels banished, an exile
climbing a mountain of dishes
and every tile seems to add
to the impending landslide of her life.

The cook, forearms covered with a cobweb
of tattoos, his mother and the Marines
inked in his flesh.
He smiles at the girl and I hear death
speaking, craggy, impenetrable, intimate.

◆

I grow thin, my beard greasy and loose.
I read somewhere that Jesus is black
and I tell a friend who turns blue.
I imagine myself a blue marble
rolling all night under doors
and through gutters hoping
to become a child again.
I watch the flowers freeze into crystal
and crumble like pins.
I bunch the blankets around me in the car
and *I am still alive.*

My waitress drives me to the sea
where I can spend the winter wrestling shadows,
where I can read Lear
to a crippled sparrow whose one note
chirps *free me, free me now*
and I won't, I won't free anything.
I will cough blood into a napkin
and wonder at death's indecision,
having lived my whole life
trying to define the lie.

◆

From the porch of my cottage,
I can see the dune with its hairpiece
of dying grass, where the historical
marker says that Sir Walter
had parked precisely there,
shouting to the mother country
like a maniac that settlers were starving,
already forefathers lay folded in shallow graves
and here I wait, Elizabeth, my wife,
my Queen, like a weed I wait.

He spent the rest of his days
kicking like a crab between her fingers,
dredging the kingdom of South America
for El Dorado's gold.
He shouted form every belfry in Britain
that he knew where the riches lay.
He shouted all the way to the guillotine,
disbelieving that his countrymen
could quiet one who loved them so,
reducing his legacy to a staring skull
rolling from the blade in silence,
having lived his whole life
only to see it ended with a lie.

PILGRIM

He couldn't outlast the everyday evil.
Alarms bleated like sheep.
Streetlights fell behind him
and he didn't care.
Bewildered ornaments dangled at the fair.
He passed them giggling.
He laughed and slapped his belly.
He scratched his face into ribbons
and passed them out.
Children ran away, hysterical with joy,
rainbows in their hair.

Hyperbole rode up and handed him a name.
He turned it over slowly in his hands,
squished it like bread dough,
plucked and plucked and made a pile.
The pieces shrieked and ran
like mice into the dark.
A weary cat was waiting there,
lapped up the syllables and mewed for more.
Love froze his sound and he cracked like ice,
rose like a frost on the air.
The dark cat never moved.
She didn't dare.
Love was suspended, glistening crystal silver
on each black hair.

Morning broke like an itch
and they stirred as one muscle,
our pilgrim and his pet.
He was liquid and licked her into shapes,
onyx eyes, tangled fingers.
They hardened together and grew,
water for her mouth,
and a root leaped out,
plunged into the earth again and again.
Split, two shapes rose blinking and stared.
What was missing sucked reason from the sun.
They stood, moaning and mirrored,
delighted at the damage they had done.

▲▲▲

THE ZOO

▼▼▼

"And those that are hunted
Know this as their life
Their reward: to walk

Under such trees in full knowledge
Of what is in glory above them,
And to feel no fear...."

"The Heaven Of Animals"
—*James Dickey*

KOKO

A small boy in a sailor's hat
sits in the square
at the center of the zoo,
ignoring the leisure suits,
surrounded by the screeches
of toucans and the laughter
of monkeys.

He buries his face
in a boat of watermelon
and rears back,
covered in a red pulp,
spitting jewels of shiny wood.
On a rock, circled by iron bars,
a gorilla is talking to a woman,

nectarine yogurt smeared on their faces
and poetically the black lips say,
"more orange flower sauce, thank you,"
reaches with a gigantic mitt
for her kitten, a manx without a tail,
fit in your fist, All Ball.

The urge to intervene is obvious,
like a lunge to block the baby
stumbling toward a swimming pool.
But Delmore's clumsy bear was an imbecile
compared to Koko, making puns,
reading, tattling, understanding

a human love and death,
using a napkin, saying please,
glancing in the Gentlemen's Quarterly
at the underwear,
wondering where the hair went.

All day Koko and Dr. Penny chat
about candy and baby oil and hats,
disregarding the heavy breath
that clanks hoarsely out
or the impatient claws
squeezing harder than expected.

The jokes are done by sunset,
when the parachute of night
settles like velvet in the pen,
when Koko climbs deep into her tree,
licking the dew from the leaves,
listening to the smaller animals

scuttle in their cages,
nibbling the remnants of rotten fruit.
Then Koko's restless mind
floats like a shark across the zoo,
hearing the blood of the good doctor
and her husband knocking and knocking
in their shifting green sheets.

The same way a warm nut of alcohol,
rattling in Theodore's belly,
rocked him down in the soft sea,
shedding his ape-like body at last,
leaving him sleek among the voices of tuna,
sliding through their pale lunar light.

Never to set the beast
chasing its own shadow, voicing out loud
the savage blood's obscenity,
only curled like Koko
in the warm hair of the night,
life-saving symbols
caked like Seconal in her mind.

YEAR OF THE SNAKE

for Arthur Dove

If a red tree could hold fire
in its fists
    and dare sun
to come down
    and claim it,
then the mercy of yellow
would not be sickness,

it would be gold.

Reclusive power greasing the tracks
for extreme grace,

    stirring the need
to rush headlong,

    breathlessly
out of this ghetto bed,
with the best view of the city,

a poverty of tales to tell.

Peasants of pleasure, rogue scientists
swooning from pure detachment,
we barter with beauty
    and hunger
until the boundaries distort,
and the orchid
       bursts
into a firework of retributions,
the asphalt yawning
    larger than before,

my sad animal erect in me.

Teenage Mutant Ninja Turtles

Nourished with nuclear love,
their story is a blur
of special effects
and space-age cartoons,
oozing terrified luxury.

Heavy metal doves,
their hearts stuffed
with steroids and acne cream,
they say, chains swinging,
I will be whole,
a grown, mature adult,
financially secure,
respected by my peers,
their pistols shivering with poise.

Rubber pajamas
and hopeless agendas
bounce them awake,
miles from weeping.
Their insomnia
is velvet and empty,
like an elevator of glass
bound forever to its building.

Suspicious icons unfold,
draping their junkie veins
across the windows
of these eyes.

NOAH

Night after night the Dog Star
swam across the sky
and Noah guzzled his homemade wine,
sleeping light in his tent,
decrepit memories invading his rest.
The faces floated past,
the faces of neighbors
that had helped to nail a roof,
blazing eyes lost forever
as the houses were swallowed by the sea.
Mile after mile, those faces
spread across his salty lawn,
parallel to the ark,
the straight lips frozen in a plea,
a barrier between the scuffling beasts
and the promise of Ararat.

If remorse is the rust of loyalty,
then out of the nothing that cradles the mind,
a brutal despotism was born.
Sweet drunken Noah,
sprung upright in the angry water of his sleep,
his chest heaving.
He waited for the sandals
to slap quickly away,
but the sand remained silent,
and the wind whipped "no"
into his throat,
"no" to form the new bastille,
"no" the fiber of life,
and the rivers receded, singing no no no,
and the streams, stripped of understanding,
begged forgiveness from the trees.

Elephant Graveyard

In the East they want an end to the rain.
Water is killing us, they say.
Across the hall, thirty squirrels
are chattering in unison,
"Jesus' love is bubbling over," they sing,
over and over,
overwhelming the day's quiet poetry,
an insistent rain
and its rooftop harmony,
filling the gutters and polishing the street.

I want them to sing;
Make me a storm, Lord
make me a storm
a giant mountain-altering gust of noise.
Let me blow out the windows
and ruffle the hair.
Let me flash forward with my head high,
waltzing down Half Moon Street today
without shame,
all my secret histories intact.

How we crave rational companions,
a lucid algebra
to combat this sudden twilight alone.
We need to know
that beyond the high windows
there are choices, that x and y
are as familiar as husband and wife,
that even in the red sky
as the sun melts to nothing,
we won't just lie in bed, regretting,
naked, a tiny prayer on our tongue.

But we never know where to go
to die, or why,
why we should feel the spirit spill
through the soles of our feet
and seep into the earth
to protect the bones of our brother.
All across Europe, after World War I,
whole fields, acres and acres of battleground
were covered with poppies.
Blood poppies, the villagers said,
fertilized with the lives of virile young men
and cultivated with hatred.

I say, pray for beautiful accidents.
Pray that the seed of your life
might blossom like the soul of an elephant,
heeding the ancient chant of the herd,
calling you home into the earth's rich peace,
where the color of chaos is ivory,
and ivory all that is left
of wandering and dark defenses
and tense unfinished journeys,
when the spinning mind
was always an inch too low
to roll with joy on the wind.

THE BLUE HOLE

"Everything is a miracle. It's a miracle
that we don't dissolve in our baths."

—*Pablo Picasso*

I awaken in the same clothes, third day,
a different canvas with the same paint.
A caterpillar lopes across my finger
and falls seventy stories to the floor.
He rolls over unfazed,
inches toward the door.

My eyes barely open, I look outside
at blurry Amarillo, mosquito derricks
punching their needle beaks into the earth.
A cowboy passes my window,
stares for a second, then smiles,
carefully tips his hat.

Somewhere far off, I hear a methodical
beating of wings, disturbing the mission bell's
perfect orb of silence.
An ice cream truck crawls, jingling
through a purgatory of empty houses,
its carnival organ moaning, low & demented.

A young priest pauses, listening,
framed by the mission door,
embroiled in the day's one respite,
a question as simple as an icy apple,
a delicious conundrum dogs him,
even the tiniest pleasure, a struggle,
a dichotomy of delight.

Tenderly,
he drops his somber vestments on the steps.

2

Riding with Lamar,
bound for the city of angels,
seven joints, a case of Corona,
and the whiskey bends.
Parked in the Painted Desert, almost midnight....

Weary of company,
we listen intently to the strings of trails
interfacing behind an avalanche of tourist shops.

In the distance,
a noose of stars being fitted for us,
a meteor's half-hidden face
leers brightly and dissipates.

The car smolders,
emits a cloud of steam,
trying to catch its breath.

Once this land,
the theatre of the dunes,
was an ocean floor
and cartoon logic
sparked the fish.

Now, cradled in the locomotion of darkness,
the senses liberate themselves.

On the horizon, shadow mountains
like monstrous ships, drift placidly away.

Two cactus bow, as if to dance,
curled in parenthesis,
punctuating the desert's constant whisper,
wind and sand,
a spiny ration of light.

3

My aunt said I was a weird child.
The animals talked to me.

In a clearing between the trees,
I made a parlor, a refuge
where the squirrels spun in circles.
The terrapin drank water from my bowl,
his head flicking gently
in and out like a penis.

Behind us, from the brush,
pheasants would burst into bloom.

After a time,
I grew to love most
the animals that did not appear.

4

The animals are still.
The desert, tranquil as a womb,
receives us without penance.
Ancient cliffs stare, their suffering silent,
and my past, a skinny arroyo
poisoned with grand gestures,
rolls before them.

My bright bird sings no more.

She was a hole filled with a crescent,
its chaotic rhythm carved her
half-promise, half-hatred
and she opened without me.

The red gate flared, growing,
and she opened,
her hands
her mouth
her mind.

She was an edge exploding,
a brilliant prism of feathers.

5

I stand like a bobby at this death hole.

Blinded for an instant by the negative space,
I deteriorate, rag of flesh swinging on a string,
A spoke flapping in the tempest, puppet to God.

I contain wells, pockets of destruction,
juices of the kings reduce my food to acid.
All is consumed, running down my legs,
eagle scream born to trumpet secrets,
my feet dancing the sundance faster & faster,
faces rise on my skin.

Content to be volcano, I hide and ignite,
hide in the earth's core and emerge,
flower of fire, roll to the sea, new earth,
island of deformity doomed to change,
a pure dirge of paper violins and children.

Drum boils into dream, tiny sensations
like the fins of baby fish brushing my loins.
I dream the dead roads melt at this post,
flashing in my teeth like the tails of comets.
I dream power made blood, tiger made butter,
the dilated eagle eye the instant of the kill.

There is no gradual progression, only the plunge.
I take my first steps, right foot, left foot,
train whistle rushes through my sleepy limbs
like lava, a shaft of sound

    O sweet darkness

      I disappear

        Now

6

Someone else is singing with my breath.

I told Amy to respect the energy of furniture,
to couple the coffee table with the couch
in the yard, let them gain a working relationship
before you marry them to the house.
Let them feel the misunderstanding
of the sun's voice. Let them know
that light is flawless and cruel,
that they will find themselves
nestled together in the darkness
when we have gone
and enjoy the fit of the other,
discovering that they have become
a set, a unit, a family, a room.

In our absence they will measure their riches.

7

I remember the first time I heard a skunk sing.
1969, staying up late
because mother said I could
because men were going to walk on the moon
she said.
I packed up my Oreos
and my cup of Pepsi
and I went out under the sky
among the heads of cabbage
buried up to their chins
with their eyes closed.
And I kept walking
toward the trash heap
where my father
let me set the grocery bags on fire
and big leaves of ash would spin
over our heads into the trees.
And then I saw them
a mother skunk and two babies.
She was singing a skunk song
high and clear and happy
scarcely disturbing the debris.
She had found a discarded pack
of shortbread cookies
barely molded and still sweet
and her children sat
nibbling their treasure while she sang.
Her head thrown back
at once into the stars & yet with them
a song that seemed to calm the air
singing to jewels she would never swim among
whose names she could not know.
She never knew I was there
I was too charmed to move
and her song stayed with me
when I returned to the house
and the TV kept saying one small step
one small step
and my father said that's horseshit
it looks like the desert
and the men hopped slowly
in dandelion suits on the moon
and my mother looked at me
and cried and hugged me tight
and my stomach felt funny.

8

Every shoulder-slung radio alters the world.

A round man with a red Strat
is teaching me the blues,
as if you could teach the blues to anyone
like geometry, as if you could buy
*The Otis Redding Handbook of Disparate
Emotional Creativity*

and just *emote* in three minutes or less,
like the method actors imparting
to their students;
Honey, just remember a day
when you were exceptionally heartbroken,
when your brain was a wasteland
and just *be that,* you know?

I think of the young intellectual drifters
crisscrossing the country for no purpose
except to fashion their own path
inside the air, the faces on the clocks
in each city, on every Big Ben replica,
infinitely interesting.
The same weight instructs them
that lashed the shoulders
that sang,

"Ahm tired of dis mess,
O Lord, so tired of dis mess."

They cannot be re-invented.
They can only lift a naked commotion.
They can only sit, as my father did,
staring for hours into his empty hands,
except my father couldn't sing.

9

The sun creeps up,
light suddenly washes the borders away.
three hawks row soundlessly overhead
like perfect pavonine beads,
weightless and unafraid.

Daily they withstand lightning hosannas,
crosswinds, whiskers of shells
from bored farm boys,
but the circle remains unbroken,
the search steady.

Forced to translate the invisible,
the poet conjures pure furious miracles,
each kiss becomes the taste
of mad communion
and incestuous revolutions
crowd his brain.

He circles, looking for signs,
anything to support his belief,
a burning barn, a two-headed newt,
a meteor trail that lingers until dawn.

He spills over sidewalks.
He peers into graves.
Ancient lives press up like daffodils
and explode in his face.

He raves and pouts,
exhilarated and horrified
wears his finest clothes in the rain
while his work flops clumsily behind him
like a bag of blood,
and he cannot stop or scream or change.

Let me fall then,
when I have become
a bitter gas seeking flame.
Let me fall
calmly
my final time,
a single feather broken
from the back of a gull,
quietly subservient,
with words
gentle enough
to heal the wind.
Let the deranged angels scrutinize,
keeping their ledgers as I float,
one more trembling arrow
lost in the blue hole.

EDEN AGAIN

Bouncing and chirping in code
across the acre of this lawn,
two cardinals, man and wife,
a small wren hoarding five eggs
in a holly bush, one terrified grouse,
and a blue jay whose name
belies his Manson-like character.
You can warm a man's life
with a good name.
The lean dogwoods hang fat
with white blossoms.
The violets open their eyes
and peer about.
In the beginning, God saw a million
beginnings, and whispered two things
in Adam's ear as he withdrew
his bloody fingers and a rib
lay writhing on the grass.
"Ample time," he whispered, "ample time,"
and then the bad joke that sank the Titanic.
Adam ignored the latter, already he busied
himself with the growing rib,
larger and larger, round and soft.
Adam's flesh shrieked in its chains.
You know the rest.
Downstairs my sister is playing the piano
she has neglected for years.
She is heavy with her first child, a boy,
who will grow to learn the trials
of his namesake, Adam,
the world's first farmer.
Even now the enzymes are swirling like liquor
around him, fitting his tongue
with the high-pitched accents
of tradition and ignorance.
If love is man unfinished,
if the gestalt must twist into a name,
let the coterie heroes of Soweto and Tibet
learn to love this one, as old as the earth.
Let them bless this boy
with the resilience of flint,
the spirit of hollyhock,
blessing his persistent name,
too beautiful to bear, too fierce to perish.

The Orchard and The Lash

Situation fluid,
the days of innocence are done.
In the month of weddings,
I borrow money to abort
my latest incarnation.
The Cycles of the Universe whir & splinter
into neon placards bearing my name.
Shame eats my poetry.
Inside the halls,
I reel like a blood-crazed piranha,
little butterscotch man
chasing a Pooh Bear God.
I growl my worship in all directions.

For a thousand years,
I wandered in the orchard
and felt the lash,
before the leaves changed
and my blood shrank back.
I am a shadow.
I pad along behind my furry creation,
sniff the honey incense
of his breath,
place my feet carefully in his tracks.

I stumble through my shedding skin,
my past lives stacked upon a pyre,
smoke retarding my transformations,
obscuring the words
that would call up the dead,
while my cartoon
bounces from tree to tree,
singing tomorrow's song,
tomorrow's poem,
a perfect candy in his head.

THE HORSES

Across the trestle and down
into the mist-drenched field,
between the autumn trees drooping
red and yellow, I shuffled slowly
until I stood in the bowl of the valley,
waiting for the horses to race the train.
They milled roughly about, watching me,
nuzzling one another, gnawing at the crystal
blades of grass, standing one hoof
on its jagged edge, like children
unsure of their pirouette.

Their hostile heads swung side to side,
at odds with my intrusion, and then
they forgot about me. The steel ribbon
came coughing from the fog,
snaking through the stony light,
clacking steady, gaining speed,
far from the tentative boundaries
of dusty stalls. They became percussion
and thunder, rising and falling
shoulder to shoulder,
free from mindless routine,
heaving like a storm.

Knotted metal was wrapped about the conductor,
like brass around a sound. He pulled
on his whistle and blew a piercing scream
to spur them on, to contest the ice in the air.
They seemed beings flooded by cream, bulging,
skating across the ground like runaway sleds.
Their lungs filled with helium, their eyes
white with challenge and with blood.
They hardened and rose glistening
like arrowheads, clawing into the clear space

where lightning sticks its tongue into the bay
and silver herring flare to the surface
like nickels in a cloud.
The conductor laughed and yelled
as the horses bore down, strained to match
the relentless rhythm of his wheels,
before a departing whistle left them defeated,
and they scattered into the trees,
the steam from their nostrils
frosting the wind, their huffing and prancing
filling the forest with ghosts.

I paused there, on the rim of the pasture,
thinking of the waiter in the club car,
pouring a string of drinks,
shaken not stirred, slapping someone
on the shoulder, asking,
O man, did you see them bastards run?
I thought of the people
floundering from the station
and into their cars,
fixing their ties, setting the time,
the rusty pipes in their apartments
singing like the train.

I thought, if I were to lose my arms & feet,
if walking slowly home I was seized
and fell paralyzed to the ground.
If wishes were horses,
I could never make them fancy verse.
I would, I thought that day,
be infected with their reckless power
in narrow threads of fiber and shell,
stitched through the framework of my bones,

as the soggy landscape sang to me
burning music borne of sorrow & experience,
crude and unfettered, a dire moan,
a confederate death
making an orchestra of a man,
forever running, forever singing back,
giving me the strength
to walk as an equal among the horses.

THE MIND AS FALCON

If I could what I would choose is silence.
But every thought breeds two tribes.
The falcon mind assaults all canary thoughts
singing between the poles of its world,
a remedy just or unjust
with the swift silver slashing
of the guillotine & the scalpel,
when imagination is held in secret tribunals
and the soul's insurrection
hatches a million pseudonyms.

I won't wrap this in cellophane.

Just the velocity of living,
solarized by fountains of light,
the heat troubling me with its butter breath,
I want to flood my waking love
with poison, with black,
to kill & kill again
and yet, standing in sooty water
with fish nibbling the bread
of my toes, praise rushes through me,
fills me like a prancing iris
& I spout gusts of blue ecstasy,
a breath only the whales know.

This is a temporary aneurism, I am told.
I am still a child. The Mardi Gras races about.
I leap-frog toward a forest of phantom trees,
spreading a death glaze on the ripening cherries.
I pirouette on a high-wire of rain
caught in the brain-defying battle of gravity.
What is to come, I haven't the tools to change.
I say, open the windows, let me sharpen my teeth
on the willow, infect my marrow with pain.

I am learning to love my rage.

▲▲▲

THE ASTROLOGY OF LONGING

▼▼▼

"The grey sheep came. I ran,
My body half in flame.
(Father of flowers, who
Dares face the thing he is?)

As if pure being woke,
The dust rose and spoke;
A shape cried from a cloud,
Cried to my flesh out loud.

(And yet I was not there,
But down long corridors,
My own, my secret lips
Babbling in urinals.)"

"The Exorcism"
—*Theodore Roethke*

THE DOOR

I cannot see the brazen denials,
or face the dreamtigers
asleep in the other country,
thunder informed by drama,
the message the salmon receive,
informed by spirit,
punctured by frozen stars.

I am covered by schools of shadows,
their dark fins deliberately curious,
cutting through the air I breathe,
growing in number as the water grows
silver with salmon, again & again,
over the dam, through the tubes,
feverish & bloated with expectancy.

They scrape through the gates,
slamming toward the door,
the door that mysteriously
swings open and I shut,
that opens and I slam,
closing my eyes that I dare hope,
and I cannot be born.

QUICKLY NOW THE CROWD

We pull the disease wagon
like tired mules.
We stop & go round the bones of the dead.
Freud was the death of sex
saying eight singers surround two lovers
in their rocking bed.

Now lovers are dying.
Yesterday a hundred whales were found
stranded in the yellow sand,
drowning in the salty Eastern air,
flippers struggling like wings
in the gravity the earth forgot.

The crowd gathered quickly,
while a few men strained to push
one of the clumsy gods,
black as sleep, back into the sea.

The largest ones were posed behind children
for scale. Photographs snapped,
beaches closed, Coast Guard called in
to find reasons, get a closer inspection.

It was as if the bowels of the ocean
were torn out & thrown steaming on the beach,
but the reports found nothing unusual.
For a time, the great beasts had grown tired
of the squid & eel squirting thru the reef's
many homes and leapt into a new sky,

celebrating a sorcery brighter than themselves.
The people carried stories of the apocalypse,
when the end was near & giant fish
crawled onto the land
making a tragic carnival of their lives.

The hammering surf unlocked the white bones
of the cliffs, flooded the people's footprints,
and swallowed the enormous bodies,
transporting its dead kings back into the deep,
swollen with a knowledge too good for this world,

foretelling the cost of freedom,
the birthmarks of anarchy that break uneven
and unhindered like freckles on the skin
of history, finding their form lovely,
a shape once moved by the moon,
where God has gone to sleep.

DIORAMA

You were afraid.
Your hands trembled on my chest
like poinsettias under snow.
You were cold, you said.
But you warmed me,
held me on your tongue
and tasted my blood.
In your mouth,
I cried like a lizard.
I fell at your beauty
and begged.
I prayed that you would
forget my name,
but you could not.
You rolled me into silence.
You kept stamping thru my trees,
leaping through my dark,
until no man could frighten you,
no knife uncover us,
until my wind exploded,
and all my flowers fattened
to make your bed.

ADULTERY

This is not what it seems.
We are clumsy and young,

amateurs in the business of lying.
We sidestep the important questions,

a watermark of love, and yet,
a red sparrow flaps wildly behind your ribs.

How can we know?
We think to climb inside a sound

and discover the rhythms of escape.
Instead, we smooth each other's skin

with consolations, placate the other
with imagined moanings.

I can never love you.
I can never leave.

Let us not speak falsely of him & her.
Let us not speak.

Sometimes, the words slide
against themselves in a cannibal fury.

The distant stars appear one by one, fuzzy,
as if covered in golden hair.

WITH A FEW STICKS

We thought we could
bludgeon it down
and we did.
It lay down slow,
quiet as ivory,
smoothly shaking
like a seal.
But
it was bigger
than a seal,
cast
a mean shadow,
took a bunch
of clubs to kill it.
Some said
Revolution.
Most didn't say.
Finally, the sky
cracked open.
We postured different.
Made us
a seal thing
that had its own way.
Said leave the clubbing
to them
that earned it.
Oowee,
we giggled,
this seal thing real!
We,
breathing easy and free,
ducked in holes,
heard the word
without
a glitch.
Make me some
beauty,
with a few sticks.

MIDLOTHIAN

a poem for Halloween

The haunted things
keep their own hours.

A Mohawk with a green smile
flexes on stage,
considers himself a thrill-seeker,
runs the risk of going to bed
without brushing his teeth.

He shouts, Hey man, Yo,
see if you can cop some blow
from that frightwig
whilst I go to the car
and fuck this tub of goo.

One demure witness,
wearing an eggshell sweater,
stands guard,
flamingoes on each breast
touching beaks.

A semi-conscious boy
in a bathroom stall
mistakes his girlfriend's dying groans
for erotic ones,
raps savagely on the door
screaming give me some peace.

ECHOES

With the mind of a mannequin,
she positioned her pearls
to catch the sun.
Like a phoenix, she learned
to unpeel in a flame-cloud,
not to learn the secrets of the ash,
but she always needed a new coat.
(Agony was, making the living
worthy of a death now & then.)

In the light of a moth-beat,
or the air fish find to breathe,
he smiled and he yawned,
usually together,
and he thought that black holes
were where God stored dreams
in tiny money bags
and one of these days,
when we could get there,
he was going and get him
a money bag or two or ten
and maybe then,
she would shut the hell up
about the sun always daydreaming
in the hollows of his eyes

and dandelions following him home
and exploding on his lawn
in a shower of white parachutes
and he learned to live weary
and he listened to the sun
chime as it set
and he mumbled to the rain
in his own style
of discontented sentences
and he embraced the echoes.

ICONS BETWEEN CLASSES

Nothing new   When I called   I made excuses
In two months   you marry   a man not like me
Brown you say   I am black and white   But brown
Lasts you say   clings   Black seeps   into
Everywhere at once Brown melts warm   But white
Is a spike   takes the longest   way home

Calling   was a decision   sandwiched
Between classes   voices   friends   clouds
The parking lot   like a coin   flipped over
In their books   the wind rattled   A black man
A silver wheelchair   fingers narrow as strings
All day   rain fell   starlings flew into windows
A girl   tire black hair   stopped between steps
Above the room   searched my faces   smiled

The coil of machine steel   in the corner   spits
Drinks down   re-fills roll over   into slots   Once
You and I   scooped   a staring bird from the shrubs
Its neck was snapped   You drove wild   to the vet
It decided to die   in the waiting room   Your face
Grew quiet   You made me drive back   slow you said

The black man   the silver wheelchair   lurched
At the drink machine   the buttons   looked down
I stood to help   Life he says   a fucking B movie
Ain't it   If I had money probably   get ear disease
In a dirty jacuzzi   you know   his face curls back
We clasp hands   swap names   Nothing new   I called
I made excuses   press the button   You marry brown
The red lips climb   a dead can   drops anyway

IREZUMI

What I cannot elevate, I cover.
Every inch of unmarked flesh cries to me.
I am carnal sculpture.
The hatred of tradition pulls me erect.
The criminals are smothered
in my colored vines, breathless monuments,
raw urban poetry.
The sailors beg for me, drunken & volatile,
pronounce me code of honor.
The rebel without my decadent chic,
snarls and departs, incomplete.
Like a military parade,
I glorify and embarrass,
enrage and astound.
A tattoo is a living thing, a talisman.
So long as the body carries me,
its blood will fuel my beauty.
I am forever, a frantic vow,
eternal flower
burning birthrights in the snow.

VANILLA

This match won't strike.
I dropped the pack in the slush
and nothing sparks.
Across the gravel road, a man
I have known all my life,
has cleared a spot in the snow
and stands with his grandson,
burning the trash.
The boy's eyes are red with the chore.
He hops around the fire
like a nervous marionette,
his blue ski cap flopping side to side.

I wonder how the old man
gets wet paper to flame up,
to part like two fat red snakes,
dancing as he waves his match
like a wand.
I throw my soggy pack aside,
cross the road and tackle the boy.
His name is Travis.
Ask him his name
and immediately he holds up
seven fingers, five and two,
as if a man were named a certain way
because he lived this long.

The house I grew up in
faces us like a black glacier,
sitting quietly in the swirling flakes.
Smoke from the burning trash
follows the wind down the valley.
A fir tree, drunk from snow,
suddenly splashes across the roof.

◆

The astrology of longing was learned
when the first nova
folded into the violent light,
the way water closes over a rock
or a diving man.

I was not yet one year old
when JFK was lanced in Dallas;
but my grandmother sent all the clippings,
because, "he must be prepared to remember."
Now every time I hear Kennedy,
the bloody photos click in my head.

There is a piece of yellow plastic,
high in the pine tree behind us.
I let it ride when I was eleven,
when it was a kite,
and a deceptive wind dumped it
out of reach in these branches.
I hopped like Quasimodo on his bell rope,
until the broken string
disconnected me, taught me loss.

I hoped one day to grow
tall enough to reach it.
But grown now, I am still short,
and the yellow wing glints
like a satin sash on a moonless night,
a testimony to all I will never attain.

I growl inwardly and declare
that the naked flagpole
beside my house,
clacking like a leper,
beating its cable in the wind,
is not the saddest sound
I have ever heard.

I have been too long away.
Here, where mistakes were made,
I will become something more.
I think I will step outside myself
and watch me from afar,
rush up if need be,
and catch my falling body in my arms.

◆

My father measured the age of his children
by the height of their first Christmas tree
that he had carefully planted in the yard.
My neighbor says he can see
the edge of his life,
half-sunk in the yard outside
his own house, where the government workers
follow a bulldozer's rising wake,
like a grounded tugboat
plowing back the harbor of a road.
We watch the fire,
surrounded by the clatter
of engines and digging.

My neighbor situates his crooked smirk
between the nuggets of snow,
hissing as they dive
into the flaming trash,
the tin cans turning blue and red.
Neruda sat his whole life
beside the sea, making a fire.
Below the lights that throbbed with money,
the forgotten faces of chalk
made his alleys milky with their breath.

He wanted his poem to be a gnat,
flying into the eye of the State,
to frolic in its head,
until its limbs swelled with concern,
until the people shook the head,
saying it is only a gnat,
we never left.

Travis tires of us
and runs toward the house,
where hot chocolate waits
in a thick white mug.
My neighbor says,
all the new thinking
is the same as the old thinking.
The bulldozer groans toward
a fresh pile of earth, then turns toward us,
like an empty boat blown from the dock,
stirred by the current in a tight circle,
pointing everywhere & saying nothing.

◆

Four of the workmen stand talking
to a single worker with a shovel.
On State wages, he digs a hole
while they gesture and giggle.

At the bank, in front of the screen
of the 24-Hour Teller,
the lights blink at the front of its brain,
"Remember," and then blurbs of words
that flash too quickly
before the screen winks, "Thank You."

I want to scream at the workers.
I want to yell at the women
behind the glass of the Drive-Thru,
"Say it and be done."
I want them to moan
into their microphones
like Bessie Smith
and make the plastic flowers melt down.
I want to throw my checkbook
into the air and watch it levitate,
graceful as a hummingbird,
balanced at last.

I want to rise up like a bloated fish,
with the soldier that crawled back
to save his friend,
toward the brilliant aquariums
of the Drive-Thru tellers,
where the women with damaged throats
peck softly on the glass,
croaking *you forgot, you forgot.*

Travis runs toward the house
in short choppy steps
that seem to last forever.

I catch a flake of snow on my tongue.
It tastes like ash,
but I imagine vanilla.

▲▲▲

WHERE THE WATER GOES

▼▼▼

"And that wafer-stone
which skipped ten times across
the water, suddenly starting to run
as it went under,
and the zeroes it left,
that met
and passed into each other, they themselves
smoothing themselves from the water..."

"The Path Among The Stones"
—*Galway Kinnell*

WORDS FOR THE DYING

The death of When
troubled How
and he rode to the ocean.
He didn't walk on the waves.
He didn't calm the hysterical fish
whose radar had begun to fade,
forgetting the boomerang
that defines the negative spaces.

He didn't speak.

When the sky forgot to hold the sun,
How watched it drop
like a doughnut into the water.

He watched it sink.

He stretched out in the darkness
and rubbed his feet.

He guessed that When
would come back around.
Or maybe a bastard son
had been left behind to take his place.

Maybe there was a night
just deep enough
for freedom to have filled every belly
and When might have seduced Forever
and Hope could be yanked out kicking,
too strong for Death,
Hope, with eyes wild and excited,
eyes that would know their father.

VERTIGO

Burdened with a bottle of reds
and a fifth of bourbon,
I shrank inside a final wish,
caged beneath a strangely silent
turquoise sky, not a gull
or cloud in sight, only the sea
whispering nonsense
and gruesome reveries.

Twenty-one seasons lurched inside me,
hunch-backed and monstrous,
like a camel train confused by mystics,
stumbling exhausted thru a whirlwind of ash.
I lay smoldering in the moist sand,
two days and nights,
my tiny life greasy & glazed with disgust,
weeping like a child
for the future to be revealed.

Out of this babble and fog,
broken into poetry,
I flattened on my wheel like a guinea pig
and cried out loud
for the god within,
any great placebo, any Master's hand.

The wrinkled horizon with its jagged lamps
testified for me, saying;
There is war all the time.
A poem can kill a man.
But the figures of that afternoon
solicited only wonder as they slid past
on their little cakes of ice.
Their oppressed maneuvers were filled
with a sense of something coming,
a sunrise with no equal in my memory.
My charred sight burned clearer
in the salt air.

What happened between me & the sky
I cannot say.
But I saw myself plain.
My frayed fuse untangled and left me,
naked and wet, one more delay
in the slithering decay of the sea.

My mind blossomed with possibilities,
with ideas unresolved.
The spray of that hope
exploded like a wave
and I was upright again,
no more than before, nor less,
but alive and balanced precisely,
like a bubble on the tip of a pin.

THE GIRL NEXT DOOR ALL GROWN UP

Halfway across the nation, you stare
at the printout, your head full of figures.
The monitors whisper your arrival.
Their antique eyes never leave
or intervene, but blink off and on
like Christmas trees.

On the phone, you pretend to plead,
Please come, please come.
I hate the way the mad look at me,
with their fingers in their mouths,
dissecting my eyes for some fleck of insanity.
The days rock like dominoes.

Your father saw love everywhere, *could see it,*
the last of his generation
to neglect the heritage of the heavy tree.
His mother carried a pink parasol
and carefully hid books of lesbian poetry
under the mattress.

We talk about anything, conservative friends,
the broth of our jobs, sloshing through
the swamp of time clocks and droning managers,
a bowl of oats washed down with lukewarm coffee,
sperm dried on your foot from the shower.

You ask if I'm angry still,
always the eyes gushing stone.
Then you mispronounce Roethke,
saying you could never forget me
reading him in a field with cheese and wine.

How we scattered the family of bees
that gathered in a furious cloud
and chased us to the river.
You trembling like a feather,
beneath the soothing ice of the waterfall,
screaming delightedly O God O God.

How the bells joined to your voice
on a blustery Sunday afternoon
became low and raced in leaping trills
across the countryside from the church.
And you giggled, they're calling the sheep.

We were close enough to walk home
and you tucked your fingers in mine.
They were cold and wet as we fell in step
toward the bells ringing in our heads,
like your words today in the phone,
the static rhythm of your sentences,

the same melody I felt when I was small,
gripping the bars of the merry-go-round
as the older boys pushed it faster & faster,
until my body rose horizontal to the ground
and the sky blasted round and round,
calling in ringlets of clouds.

The rusty bars creaked like broken teeth,
lifting me upon a bed of freezing air,
pulling my shirt, my hair,
beating a sour foam across my face,
lifting, lifting,
until one hand began to slip......

To My Teacher At 50

You make up stories now, tell lies
to romanticize my 'genius'.
We worry, friends call infuriated
that such things could be.
The analyst prescribes medication.
To you, there is only the mirror
and its translations,
like a poetaster with a tin ear.
There is danger beyond your door.
Friends are turncoats.
You sleep all day
and awaken to hiss at the world
like a enraged swan.
Please, my love, look into the mirror
again at the eyes, the fiery eyes
that made Blake's tiger
scamper in my mind's new jungle,
when music made a tiger's stripes alive.
There is still time for dancing,
still your hands are strong enough
to recall banging the tambourine
all evening as we sang
and you understood the thunder.

CASTRO'S GHOST

It could be said,
with Eastern Europe teetering on a ledge,
that a good man
should coax the ignorant down.
If need be, trade trinkets
for an island of promise.
But the end of this century
brews no future.
One decade rekindles another
whose glory was lost, and rightly so,
only the dead belong to yesterday.
They belong and behave.

In a world glutted with images
the artists struggle to find their own.
They swell and splinter like broken windows,
and through them I see a fire in the sky,
orange crystals leaping from underground.
In the womb of thought the earth builds ships
loaded with fruit and launches them.
Some rise like balloons & burst into countries.
The others are ice and fog,
air without color,
gone without their story being told.
Most people don't live or die, they just float.

There is an old Cajun woman,
tied together with scarves,
who wanders the beach adrift,
peering across the mists
into the Gulf of Mexico,
looking for Castro's ghost.
Because her husband,
full of fury and spiced rum,
set out away from her,
rowing through the black water toward Cuba.
He was going to assassinate Castro, he said.
He had his reasons and he left.

There are things men tell no one,
not each other, not a wife.
The mountains of the mind hold secrets
this delicate, and yet, when they rise
their knowledge can nudge us
off the mark, into the storm,
a mirror emptied of reflection,
fractured beyond repair.
There are artists who look at their work
and see nothing more to be explained,
so they lie, or they wait,
wait for that indescribable moment

when the sky gives up its own secrets
and singing ignites and absolves them.
No news, but motion at last.
At the least, that maverick understanding
that we must act and act now,
guided by a flurry of whispers
down through the littered theatre
where the dead selves perform
their dramas of resignation and regret,
listening for the tribal heartbeat,
the talking drum that steers them
all the way back into life.

DREAM TRAIL

On the map of your body,
I marked a road.
A tender path through marshes
and magnolias that droop with sleep
and brush across my windshield as I pass,
waving, as I am told the Japanese wave,
waving good-bye until their guest
is a dot on the sun, not turning away
in a rush, but waving at the memory
a handshake made, the wind
through the fingers sharing.

If I could turn a stone in you,
without the dark acids bubbling up
around my feet and lay my cheek
against the dead grass, jaundiced now,
but waiting, waiting for the spark
of a star to turn in your thighs,
the green lights to glow again
in the fields of your eyes.

At every quiet fork, you divide
your prayers into want and need
and forge ahead down a path
untangling into night,
saying grant me a respite
from what the butchers
claim to be right.
Close my eyes to the messages
laid out in the symmetry of bones.

We came together like blind roots
out of fear and in that pocket,
your teeth tick like castanets.
The moon limps behind a cloud
and rests there, a humming stone.
In the night of your answer,
the gonging of our blood will be told.
On the map of your body,
I marked a road.

Twilight In Brooklyn

I tell myself, learn to enjoy the world,
and I do.
I give a glint to the sharp rain.
I give away everything.
Determination Hope Release
I give the toll
that springs from several names.
Perfect Bedlam, of course,
is the easiest and first to know.

We were a sunflower and a scarecrow.
We kept the blackbirds laughing.
Through the branches darkly we unfolded.
Our great black wings covered the sky.
We flew to the top of the mountain
and took a swing on every tree.
We gave Justice its venom
and ignored the law.
We perched on love's impropriety.

Sometimes heroes cannot see to see.
We were a parka
protecting Lenny Bruce from the stares.
We were a soul finger wagging in the air.
We were trembling in a bottomless wind,
the tenants of a swollen conspiracy,
too much and too little, afraid to grieve,
afraid that any gust of doubt
might strip us of our wings.

We were interrogated by whippoorwills
that drummed us with Swinburne
when Whitman crossed our minds.
With boundaries and violent perfume
we paid for our appetites.
We were minnows dressed in black
seeking communion.
All our nightmares were important.
They forged our slippery alliance
and made despicable past mistakes
simple to digest.

What became of us was winter
and the trickle of inaction,
the scent of harvest interrupted
and pearl white skin.
There was silence spreading & explicit carnivals,
coming together as we were on a gamble,
with dangerous holy decrees,
beggars on a blue bridge
under salmon clouds,
kneeling at the wall of denial

a pink twilight all around.

WHERE THE WATER GOES

"The river was the abundant belly
of beauty itself..."

I love darkness
the way Monet loved water
its eddies and swirls
its secret agendas
the unbroken ladders of escape

I trickle out
a phrase in a grand dialogue
arrested by unprincipled
unbearable loneliness
that makes me
wonder what I am

And I am reminded
that the poet is a willow
bending gently down
to drink
from the world's flashing stream

Curled in half-sleep
handicapped by rage
I slip away to drink
the toxic Gotham morning
Throbbing taxis race below
and above
wrestling with God
two lovers moan deliciously
in the river of their bed

Awakening
how many structures
of reality within the river
each radiance
a separate soul
drifting
some matchless accident
forgotten

•••

On the corner
stands a beggar
with a fiddle
playing Brahms
paper cup between his feet
the sun sad and gray
on a string
behind his head

Black cabdriver
sings a Persian song
smiling
motions me inside

He
is the river
The
river is his song
a rippling opulent shell
washed
by ancient whispers

She-goat stumbles
from the alleyway
bones
clanking
in a bag
Halo of hair
settles
all around her

a festival

•••

Lives
jumble and lurch
in Soho
14 masks confronting death
dreaming of Gaugin
All alone
in the descent of hope

Fortunes dismissed
as fairy tale
window dressing
mosaics
of the catacombs

The
Hotel Dorset
leans down
a puzzle of appetites

Above
the museum
the students
are hypnotized
missing their coffee
forgiving
their flesh

delighted

•••

Kerouac's strange red afternoons
spark
from the windows
of the planes
that hang
like flies
overhead

nowhere
to
go
but
down

I
totter
home
like a tarantula
with the memorized steps
of a Southern gentleman
minding the family manner

those sad sullen regiments
bunched
like muscles
between
the mountains
and
the sea

Only a man who knows
his prison
can pitch & wail
at the gates
of his lover

Struggling
to swim
back

to
the shore
of his birth

the forgotten
bliss
of
that
blind
helpless
extreme

•••

Hallucinating
in
Amy's bed
limitless meadows
of
sensation
exchanging histories

removing the third mask

With enough love
I
could construct
a sky
that would churn
us
into
lightning

golden snakes
striking
at shadows

Come
she says
to dream
and to know

are one

In her eyes
I see
the tender
gypsy
courage
that tempted Lorca

I want
her
to cry

plush unhindered tears
of
joy

●●●

Like a bull
in winter
I push
the
river

until the windows
stiffen
with
our breath

until
the house

alive
with
the fragrance
of
frightened horses
&
delicate rain

blurs

The river descends
a tangled
spiral
repose

In the darkened street
a shadow
sobs
quietly

Humping
a sack
of cans
toward the grocer

•••

Stoned
on
the
staircase

smoke rings
flap
their manta fins
&
fly skyward

Taxi Driver on cable
mesmerized
as
De Niro dismantles N.Y.

Red-haired angel
in
Washington Square
dreaming
of
razzmatazz
in plaid

sinking into cloud

wondering
aloud
at the fountain

just where
all
this water
could

go

This book was produced using
QuarkXPress on a Macintosh.
The body typestyle is Stone Serif;
titles are set in Device.